LEARN YOUR FRETBOARD

Tips & Techniques

THE ESSENTIAL MEMORIZATION GUIDE FOR GUITAR

LUKE ZECCHIN

FRETBOARD MEMORIZATION WORKSHOP

If you like this book, you'll love the workshop!

This online master class gives you the benefit of sitting down with a real teacher, while maintaining the flexibility of learning at your own pace. Here you'll be guided step-by-step through the key concepts, techniques, and exercises needed to master your entire fretboard—quickly and easily. This is your shortcut to demystifying the fretboard puzzle! For more information, head to **LearnYourFretboard.com**.

This book is dedicated to my son, Theodore. May music find you as it has found me.

ISBN: 978-0-9925507-2-1

Published by **GuitarIQ.com**

Copyedited by Allister Thompson

Proofread by Dan Foster

Illustrated by Jasmin Zecchin

Contents

Get Your Free Online Bonus Now!

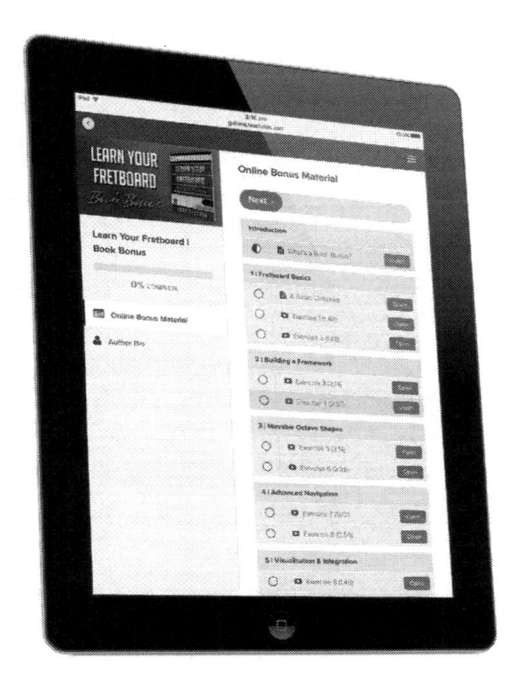

This book comes complete with free online bonus material. We've compiled a companion website to enhance your reading experience. Extras include audio examples, backing tracks, bonus downloads, and more!

Get your free bonus content at: **www.guitariq.com/lyf-bonus**

Preface

Welcome, and thank you for choosing ***Learn Your Fretboard***.

Developing a working knowledge of the guitar fretboard is one of the simplest things a guitar player can do to help streamline and accelerate the learning process. Many aspects of learning guitar require countless hours spent developing technique and musical proficiency. In contrast, being able to navigate the notes on the guitar neck isn't a skill that's dependent on either playing ability or theoretical knowledge. With some basic insight and the application of a few key techniques, anyone can begin to visualize notes across the entire fretboard quickly and easily.

Knowing the notes on the fretboard is fundamental to everything we do on guitar. This includes finding our way around the guitar neck, naming specific chord shapes and scale patterns, or simply communicating what we're playing to others. Being able to clearly visualize the fretboard will assist us in understanding the musical context behind the things we play. It will also enhance our ability to creatively translate musical ideas to different areas on the guitar neck. A clear and practical knowledge of the fretboard that's easily integrated into real playing situations is one of the key steps toward progressing as a guitarist.

I sincerely hope this handbook helps illuminate the fretboard and uncover the building blocks for continued creativity and inspiration.

—Luke Zecchin

Introduction

Memorizing the guitar fretboard is a skill that will prove inherently beneficial to guitar players at any stage in their development. As such, despite its simplicity, the content we'll cover will be relevant to guitarists of any skill level. Although this book assumes some familiarity with the guitar, here's a quick primer on the absolute basics. Below is a brief look at four central parameters with which you should already be acquainted:

- A standard guitar fretboard generally has 22 to 24 frets.
- Each fret represents a half-step movement through the 12 notes of the musical alphabet.
- The six strings across each fret are numbered from the lowest (6th string) to the highest (1st string) in terms of pitch.
- The accepted standard for tuning these strings is: E - A - D - G - B - E.

As you work through this book, it's important to remember that the exercises provided aren't intended for developing playing technique but for practicing mental recall and visualization. Think of each exercise as a platform to help build visual connections. The important thing is developing spatial awareness, focusing on the visual relationship between the musical alphabet and the guitar neck. As such, you're encouraged to practice these types of visual exercises both with and without the guitar.

Always keep in mind that developing speed isn't the initial goal. In fact, attempting to play these exercises too fast will be potentially counterproductive. The set tempos of each exercise in this book serve only as general suggestions. All exercises should be played at a comfortable tempo that accommodates accuracy.

1

Fretboard Basics

This first chapter explores the basic structure of the fretboard and establishes a simple rule for locating any note on the guitar neck.

Refining Our Focus

The fretboard can certainly seem overwhelming at first. Just looking at the guitar neck, we're confronted by various strings, an expanse of frets, a bunch of dots, and an assortment of musical notes. That's all before we even try to play anything! Our task as guitar players is to process and make sense of all this information. Unfortunately, for many aspiring musicians, this task just seems too difficult or time consuming.

The premise we're working with, however, is that memorizing the notes on the fretboard can be neither difficult nor time consuming. Although learning anything of value requires a bit of effort, for a moment let's forget the seeming enormity of this task and simply focus on a few key aspects of what we can see:

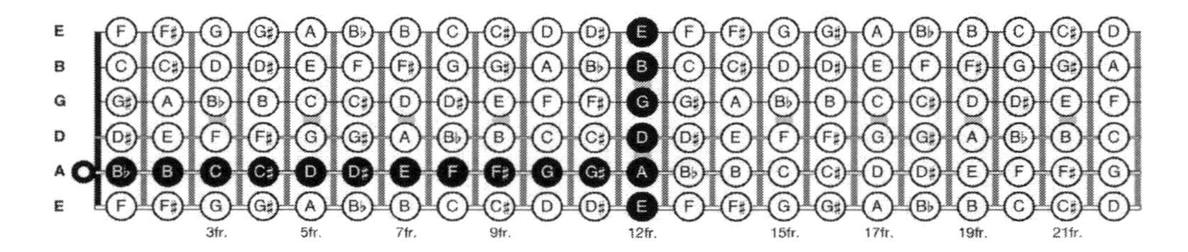

- First, although we're staring at over 130 different notes across the guitar fretboard, there's actually a large amount of repetition here. Remember, the musical alphabet has only 12 notes, and these notes repeat in a consistent and predictable fashion.

- Second, even though a standard guitar usually has 22 or more frets, we can see that the 12th fret is a direct repetition of the open strings (just one octave higher in pitch). If we dissect the guitar neck at this point, we're basically left with an identical mirror image between the bottom half and top half of the fretboard. This means learning the fretboard is only half as difficult as it first appears!

This can be consolidated further to help streamline the information we're working with. Since each fret represents a half step, all sharps and flats on the fretboard can be understood as *shared tones* between notes (e.g., G# and A♭ occupy the same fret). In other words, sharps and flats can be viewed in their proximity to *natural notes* (notes without sharps or flats). For example, if we can pinpoint F on the fretboard, by default we'll also be able to locate F#, given that the two notes are so closely related. With that in mind, it makes sense initially to concentrate our focus solely on the natural notes of the musical alphabet. This makes the task of fretboard memorization much simpler and more manageable. Notice the key things we can now observe:

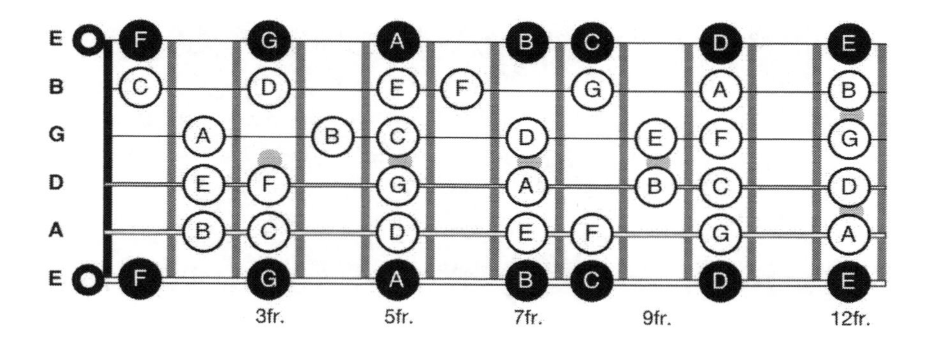

- First, if it's not already clear, the high E string on the guitar is an exact replica of the low E string. Conveniently, we're only really dealing with learning the notes across five different strings, not six. This means over 30% of the work in memorizing the fretboard is already done for us, just from learning the low E string!

- Second, the musical alphabet cycles in a consistent pattern across the fretboard. The seven natural notes move from A to G before looping back to A again. This sequence always occurs in a straightforward and predictable way. Each note simply moves up one whole step (two frets) from the last note. The only exceptions to this are between B to C and E to F. These notes are connected by just one half step (one fret).

Tip: *Another way of saying this is that every note has its own sharp except B and E.*

One Fret or Two?

The last point in the previous section is fundamental for mapping out notes across the entire guitar fretboard. Without even realizing it, we've just learned a simple system we can apply to the fretboard, with little need for brain training or memorization. Why? Because we already know the exact distance from each note on the fretboard to the next. Starting at the open strings and playing through each natural note of the musical alphabet, we're confronted by just one basic question: To play the next note, do I move up one fret or two?

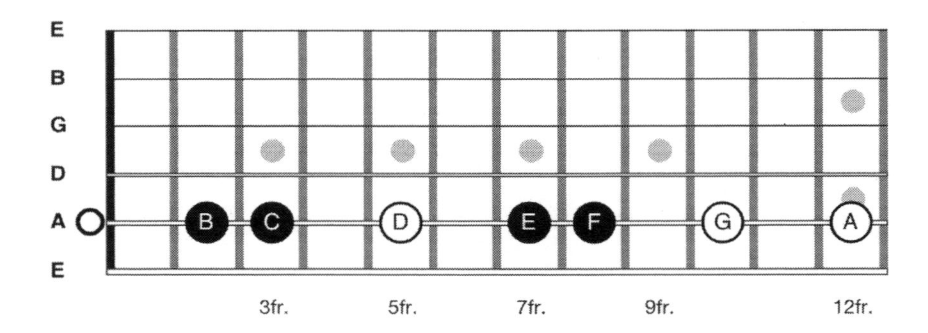

The answer is simple! Running through the alphabet, every natural note ascends by a whole step until we reach either B or E. These notes will only move up by a half step. In other words, each natural note counts up two frets, except B and E, which only count up one. For example, applying our system from the open 5th string, we know B must be two frets from A, but C will be one fret from B, and so on.

A Basic Checklist

This first chapter has revisited the absolute fundamentals of fretboard anatomy. Hopefully, these introductory concepts will already be familiar to many. In the following chapters, we'll explore more innovative and useful ways of working with this information. Before continuing, however, it's important to make sure we clearly understand the basics. Here are some simple questions you should be able to answer before moving forward:

- What notes occur across the open strings when a guitar is in *standard* tuning?
  E - A - D - G - B - E
- Which two strings share an identical sequence of notes?
  low E + high E
- Approximately how many frets are there on a normal guitar fretboard?
  22-24
- At which fret do the notes on the guitar neck begin to repeat?
  twelfth
- How many notes are in the musical alphabet?
  twelve
- How many natural notes are in the musical alphabet?
  seven
- How many notes in the musical alphabet are either sharps or flats?
  five
- Which natural notes in the musical alphabet are separated by only a half step?
  B → C E → F

Exercise 1

Move through each natural note of the musical alphabet across all strings between the open position and the 12th fret.

Playing to a metronome, start at the low E string and move through the musical alphabet until you reach the 12th fret as shown below. It's essential to name each note aloud as you go. Repeat this process on each subsequent string until you reach E on the 12th fret of the 1st string.

Example 1.1

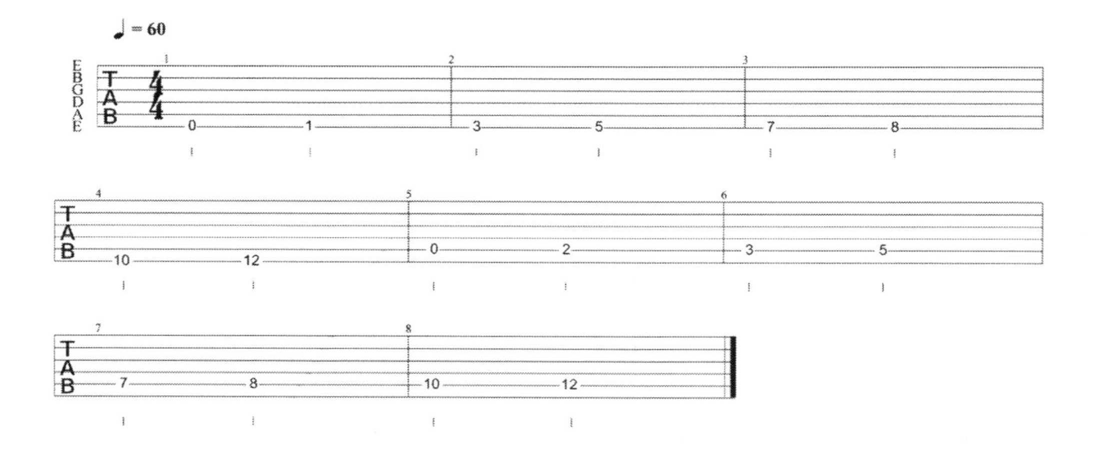

> ***Tip:*** *Although the previous diagrams are available for reference, the point is to apply the simple* ***One Fret or Two*** *rule we've committed to memory. This exercise shouldn't really require the use of visual aids.*

Exercise 2

Move through each natural note of the musical alphabet backward across all strings between the 12th fret and the open position.

Become familiar with the descending alphabetical sequence (G - F - E - D - C - B - A). Playing to a metronome, start at the 12th fret of the high E string and descend the musical alphabet until you reach the open position as demonstrated. Naming notes aloud as you go, repeat this process on each string until you reach the open E on the 6th string.

Example 1.2

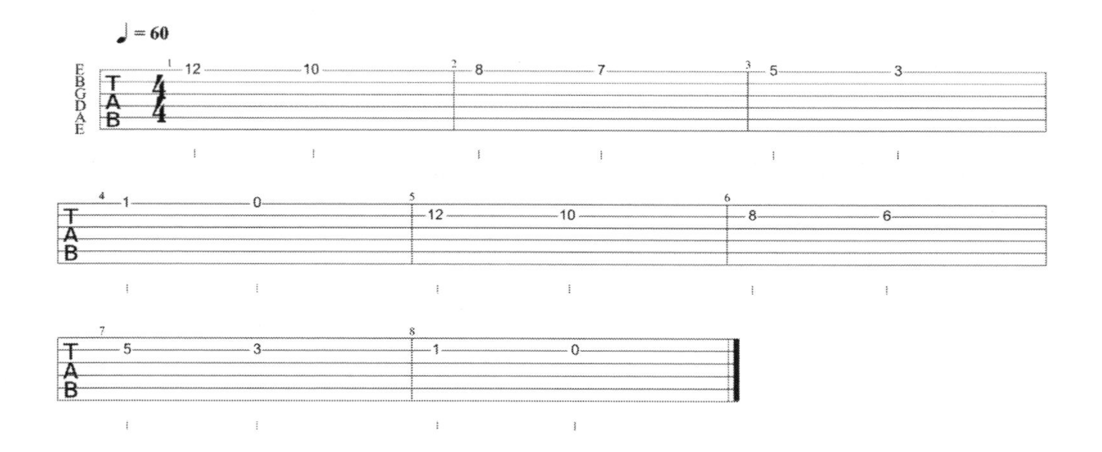

Tip: Although the system is the same, descending backward means each half-step movement now occurs after reaching every F and C note.

Extra Credit

- See if you can extend both **Exercise 1** and **Exercise 2** across the full length of the fretboard.
- Try slowly increasing the tempo of each exercise when comfortable.

2

Building a Framework

Now that we've firmly established the foundations, in this chapter we form a framework for fretboard visualization by isolating key reference points.

Location & Integration

In the previous chapter, we covered fretboard basics. We established a key method for processing and simplifying the information on the guitar neck. We then isolated a simple but effective system for mapping out all the notes across the entire fretboard. In one sense, finding different notes on the guitar is just that easy. This is perhaps why many guitar players don't move past this point. From a practical standpoint, however, it's far more beneficial to see fretboard visualization as a two-part process. These two key concepts are:

- **Location:** *Location* simply refers to the initial process of finding particular notes on the fretboard. As we've seen, this generally involves understanding how the musical alphabet is structured and how this information is applied across the guitar neck. Despite being relatively simple, however, in reality this isn't a very practical or speedy process.

- **Integration:** *Integration* is about working toward consolidating this information into our playing. We want to begin visualizing different notes, not just in their alphabetical sequence, but also in the context of their unique position on the guitar neck. This approach involves techniques for accessing this information quickly and is more consistent with how we use the fretboard practically. As such, it will be our focus moving forward.

Vertical Anchor Points

The previous chapter looked at the horizontal sequence of notes on the guitar neck. In contrast, this chapter will focus on some key *vertical* sequences. When locating notes on the fretboard, we usually resort to counting through the musical alphabet from each open string. Why? Because this is the reference point we're most familiar with. While this method may be helpful when playing around the open position, it becomes less practical the further we move up the fretboard.

There's a simple solution to this problem: We need to establish some *alternate* reference points. The open strings are a helpful anchor point because they represent a series of notes across all six strings that don't contain sharps or flats. However, there are also a few other places this occurs on the guitar neck. Besides the open position, we can see that there are vertical rows of natural notes across the 5th and 10th frets as well. Because these rows are so evenly spaced on the guitar neck, it's very convenient for the purpose of fretboard memorization. Visualizing multiple reference points is more consistent with how we'll actually use the fretboard when playing:

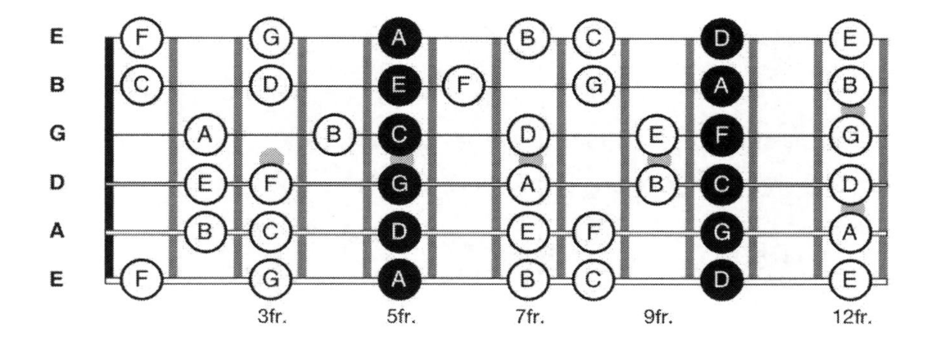

Tip: *Remember, the fretboard repeats itself, so these exact sequences can also be found on the 12th, 17th, and 22nd frets.*

Fretboard Acronyms

To reiterate, the open strings are the main reference point most guitar players are familiar with. The goal here is to replicate this familiarity using both the 5th and 10th frets. In doing so, we create a basic three-tier framework that's more easily integrated into actual playing situations. Let's take a closer look at each position in more detail:

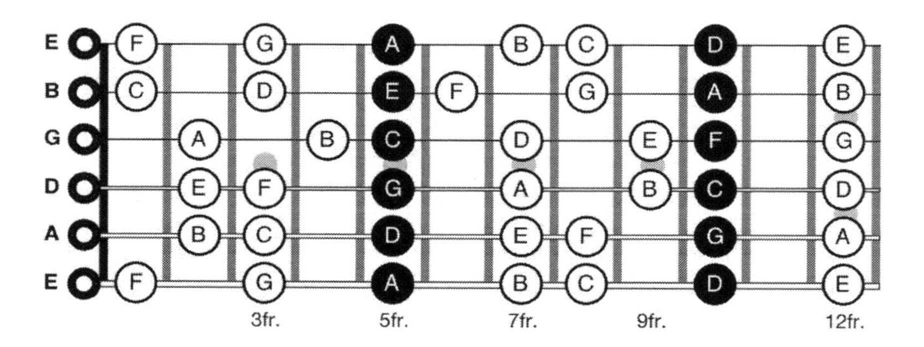

- First, we know the open strings: E - A - D - G - B - E
- Next, across the 5th fret we have: A - D - G - C - E - A
- Finally, from the 10th fret we have: D - G - C - F - A - D

Although it isn't particularly difficult to memorize a few six-letter sequences, you may find the use of acronyms helpful. While coming up with little sayings of your own is a beneficial memorization exercise, here are a few suggestions to get you started:

- **E**ffort **A**nd **D**etermination **G**o **B**efore **E**xcellence
- **A**ny **D**iligent **G**uitarist **C**an **E**asily **A**chieve
- **D**on't **G**et **C**aught **F**retting **A**ll **D**ay

Tip: *Because a key concept throughout this book is developing visual connections on the fretboard, as mentioned earlier, practicing visualization both with and without the guitar is encouraged. The ability to picture notes in our minds when we're not playing will certainly benefit us when we are playing.*

Note: For each of these reference points to be of greatest benefit, it's important that you memorize them thoroughly before moving forward.

Exercise 3

Play through each vertical reference point we've established across the entire fretboard.

Commit all three sequences to memory. Playing to a metronome, practice looping through each vertical sequence you've memorized as illustrated below. Again, be sure to name each note aloud as you go, extending this exercise to repeat at the 12th, 17th, and 22nd frets.

Example 2.1

Tip: *Because you'll also be moving backward through each sequence, be sure to memorize the notes by themselves in addition to the acronyms they create.*

Exercise 4

Divide the fretboard between each vertical sequence we've looked at and focus on the notes contained within each section.

Play to a metronome and move through each natural note in the spaces between our reference frets. Starting on the 6th string, ascend through each string between the open position and the 5th fret as seen below. Once at the 5th fret of the high E string, reverse this pattern to descend back through to the 6th string again.

Shifting to the next reference point, repeat this exercise, moving back and forth between the 5th and 10th frets. Be sure to name each note aloud as you go. There should be four notes on each string, two from the reference frets and two in between.

Example 2.2

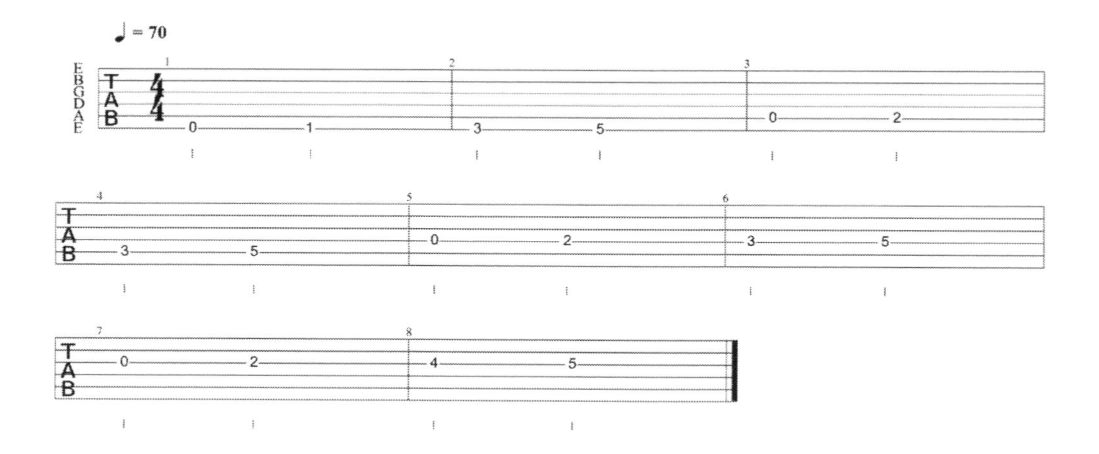

__Tip:__ Unlike the broader exercises in __Chapter 1__, this time you're focusing on specific areas of the fretboard, using vertical reference points to guide you. Notice the amount of repetition between each sequence. Try paying careful attention to the physical position of each note as you go. Remember, you want to view each note as occupying its own physical space on the fretboard, not just as part of an alphabetical sequence.

Extra Credit

- Repeat **Exercise 4** between the 12th and 17th frets and then again between the 17th and 22nd frets.
- Try modifying **Exercise 4** by alternating direction on each string as you move between reference frets. In other words, ascend notes on the 6th string, then *descend* notes on the 5th string, and so on. Reverse these directions when looping back from the 1st string to the 6th.

3

Movable Octave Shapes

Having memorized our key reference points, in this chapter we'll extend their reach by exploring various shape repetitions that occur across the fretboard.

Fretboard Repetitions

So far, we've firmly mapped out the overall landscape of the guitar neck. We then identified key anchor points to reference in the different areas of the fretboard. It's now time to focus our attention on some specific shapes that occur around any given playing position.

A central insight into fretboard anatomy is that every note on the guitar repeats within two or three frets of itself. In most cases, this repetition occurs on both sides, above and below each note. Because this happens in such close proximity, it's a very useful visualization tool that's easily integrated into playing situations.

Below we'll demonstrate what this looks like using D on the 5th fret of the A string. The concept is simple: If we skip two strings and then move *back* two frets, we arrive at the same note one octave higher in pitch. This is also true when we move *up* two frets, but this time we only need to skip over a single string:

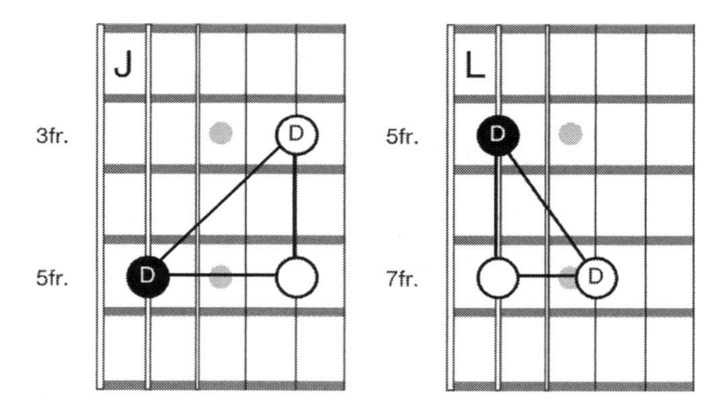

These diagonal patterns provide two basic templates that can be applied to any note. The first resembles a *J* shape, and the second forms an *L* shape on the fretboard. These patterns enable us to easily locate or cross-reference notes relative to the position we might be playing in. Next, we'll look at how these shapes can be moved and altered to function in any position on the guitar neck.

Moving Shapes

Although both shapes basically stay the same, there are a few alterations we need to make when moving them around to different strings. Let's see how the first J pattern applies to other strings:

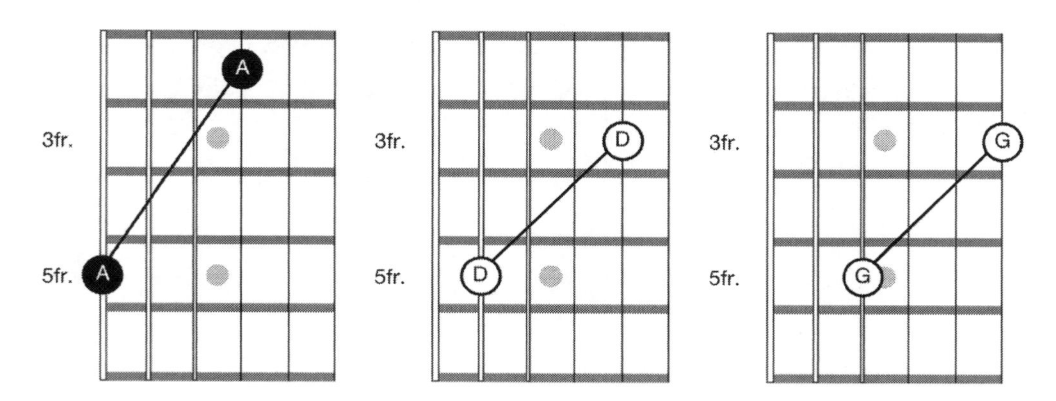

Using the pattern based on the 5th string as our template, we can see that when shifted to the 4th string, the shape stays the same. If we drop back to the 6th string, however, the shape still skips two strings, but this time it stretches back three frets instead of two.

Although these examples use notes based on the 5th fret, each shape would obviously function the same when moved up or down to any fret. Now, let's see how the second L pattern applies to other strings:

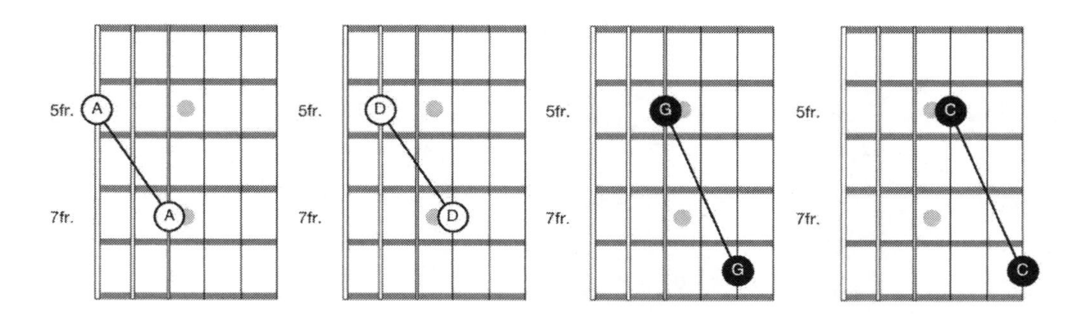

Again, if we use the 5th string pattern as our basic template, we can see that when dropped to the 6th string the shape stays the same. When shifted up to either of the higher strings, however, the shape again stretches by one fret.

Therefore, using the 5th string patterns as a template, the principle of moving between strings is fairly straightforward. In short, our octave shapes will stretch by one fret if we move either the J shape *down* to the lower string or the L shape *up* to the higher strings.

> ***Tip:** While moveable octave shapes have various uses, guitar players often reference them to track notes back to the 5th and 6th strings (which are usually the first strings memorized).*

Connecting the Dots

Now that we've established how these movable shapes function by themselves, we can begin to see how they're related to one another. It's important to recognize that none of these shapes exist in isolation. By simply locating one note, we can uncover an entire connected network of shapes. Below is an example of how each pattern works together.

At first glance, this collection of A notes just looks like one big diamond shape. However, when broken down, we can see that it essentially consists of four connected octave shapes. Our first shape is repeated in a *J* pattern from the notes based on the 6th and 4th strings. And our second shape is repeated in an *L* pattern from notes based on the 6th and 3rd strings:

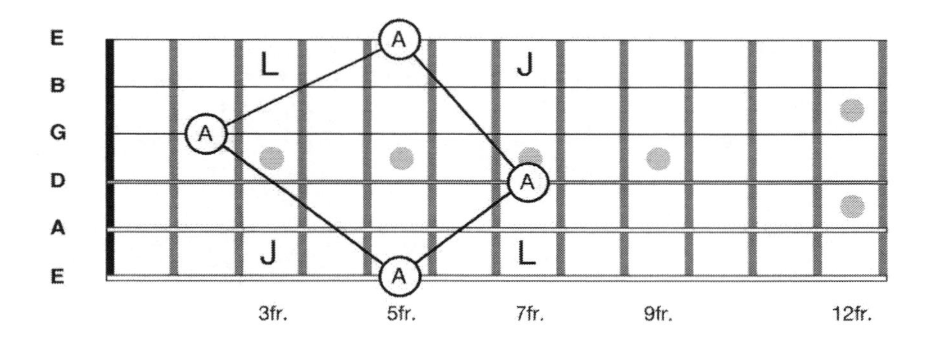

Up to this point, it isn't a coincidence that we've used examples based on the 5th fret. As demonstrated, this technique can be applied to our reference frets (established in **Chapter 2**) to dramatically extend the reach of each note within this basic three-tier framework:

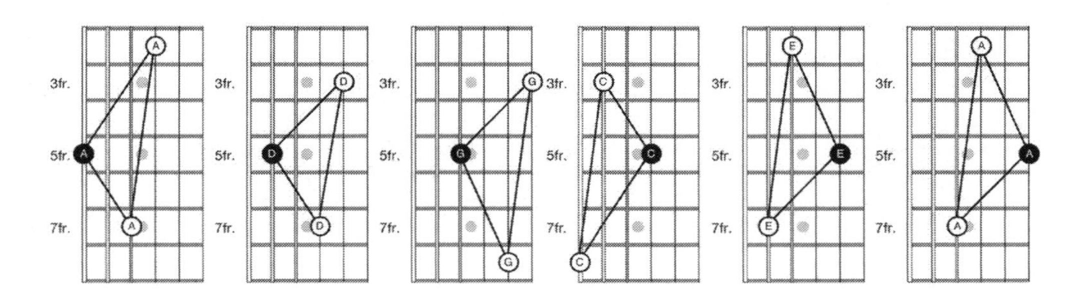

Tip: *Notice the repetitive triangular shapes each connected note grouping creates. These octave patterns work both ways, extending in one direction from notes on the lower three strings and in reverse from notes on the higher three strings. Remember, these shapes can be used to extend our reach from any of the reference frets we've memorized.*

In addition to applying these shapes vertically across any fret, it's beneficial to see that each shape also connects *horizontally* along the fretboard. As seen below, if we trace the various octaves of a single note up the entire guitar neck, we find some interesting repetitions. Far from being grouped in random locations across the fretboard, we can see the appearance of distinct sequences. This repetition consists of each single-octave shape stacked in series on top of one another:

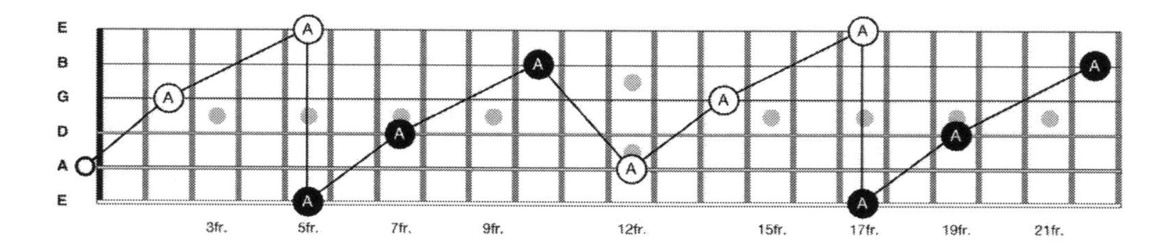

Tip: *Notice how these notes zigzag consistently across the fretboard in groups of three. Again, this pattern simply mirrors itself at the 12th fret. Although the starting locations will differ, these extended shapes will function in the same way from any note in the musical alphabet.*

Exercise 5

Using the reference points established in the previous chapter, isolate the connected octave shapes around each of these frets.

Playing to a metronome and naming each note aloud, move through the various *triangular* octave shapes across each vertical anchor point. Starting on the reference fret, cycle up and back through each note in order of the closest strings. Once back at the reference fret, move across to the next string as seen below.

Example 3.1

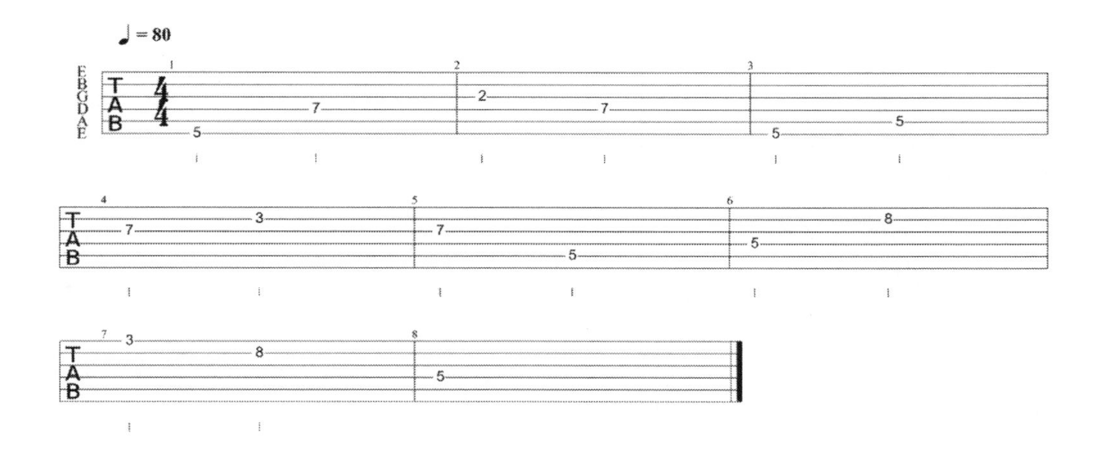

> ***Tip:*** *Remember, the triangular shapes alternate direction on the top three strings.*

Note: This exercise will only be possible across reference frets 5, 10, 12, and 17.

Exercise 6

Move from the lowest possible position on the fretboard to the highest, using only connected octave shapes.

Playing to a metronome, begin with the open A note on the 5th string and make your way to the highest possible A note on the fretboard (in terms of position, not pitch). Do this by locating and connecting each movable octave shape as demonstrated below. Name each note aloud and repeat this for every natural note from A to G.

Example 3.2

Note: Starting shapes will change depending on the location of the first note. The highest possible position will also change depending on the length of your fretboard. Where notes can be played on either the 1st or 6th strings, just play both.

Extra Credit

- See if you can play **Exercise 6** using only sharps or flats.
- Try playing **Exercise 6** in reverse. Choose any note, starting at its highest possible position on the fretboard, and descend back through to its lowest position.

4

Advanced Navigation

We've now established some foundational strategies for fretboard visualization. In this chapter, we'll explore the use of additional navigation points.

Floating Reference Points

In the previous chapter, we discussed the various note repetitions that occur around any given playing position. As an example, we looked at applying these different patterns to substantially extend the reach of the basic anchor points established in **Chapter 2**. In this section, we'll explore a dynamic approach that combines elements from both concepts. We'll highlight some broader reference points using the repetitive patterns that occur across the fretboard.

In developing this idea, let's refer to it as visualizing *floating* reference points. Not because these anchor points move, but because they're spread over the fretboard in a less linear fashion than those previously established. This is a positive thing because it closely reflects the way we actually use the fretboard, often in smaller, nonlinear note groupings.

This concept involves isolating repetitive note clusters across the fretboard. These patterns can be used to complement the other techniques we've been working with. For this example, let's isolate every B note up to the 12th fret. Using techniques discussed in **Chapter 3**, this pattern of connected octave shapes should look familiar. From here, it isn't difficult to also visualize each C note, because these notes simply occur next to one another in sequence:

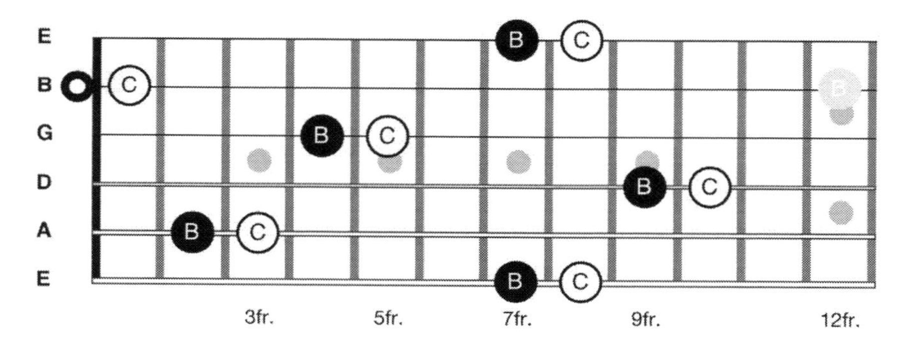

This illustrates the basic technique of visualizing connected note groupings that repeat along the fretboard. As we'll see, this concept can be extended further to make the structure of the guitar fretboard work to our advantage.

Half-Step Note Groupings

As we've discovered, the fretboard is a very repetitive and predictable beast. Therefore, in theory we could create floating reference points using any note groupings. However, it makes sense to continue with these *half-step* clusters, because they occupy a space and shape on the fretboard that's unique to any other natural note groupings.

We've already mapped out the half-step movements between B and C, which leaves us now with E and F. The technique here is the same. Once we've isolated the connected octave shapes formed by each E note, we can easily visualize each F note following in sequence:

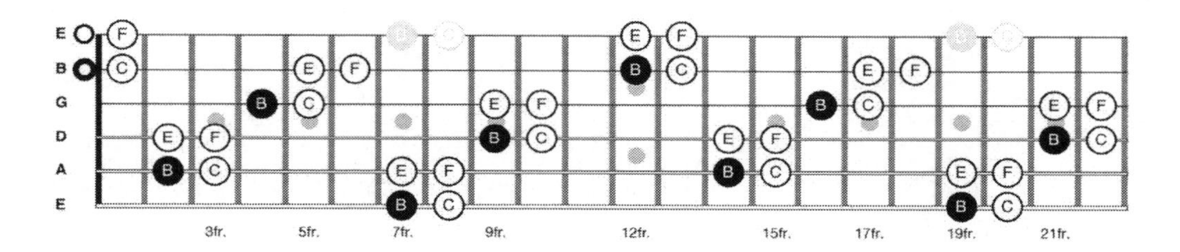

This is where everything starts making sense. As helpful as visualizing both half-step movements independently might be, the real value of this concept becomes clear when we view them grouped together. As you can see, in almost every situation the notes B, C, E, and F occur directly opposite one another on the fretboard! The only exception is between the 2nd and 3rd strings, where they're staggered by one fret.

Therefore, by isolating just one note (in this case B), we've discovered a repetitive series of connected note clusters. These basic note groupings account for over half of the natural notes in the musical alphabet!

Whole-Step Note Groupings

For an even more comprehensive set of floating reference points, we can extend this technique by adding a second shape. Using the same concept, but this time isolating each G note on the fretboard, we're able to target note groupings using the remaining natural notes. Similar to the previous section, we can see that each A, C, and D note forms another note cluster around every G note. The exception is that this time they're a whole step apart instead of a half step:

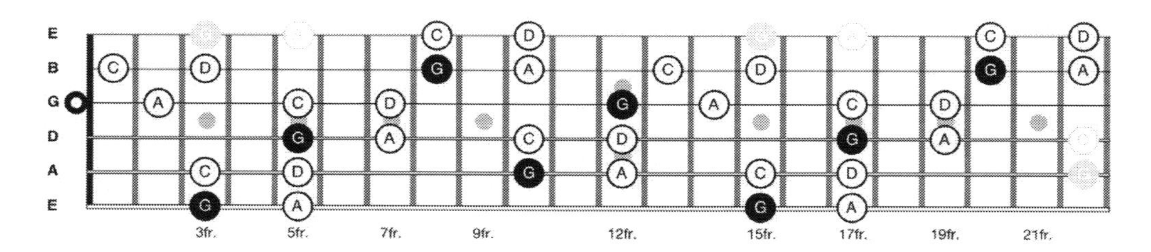

Again, in almost every situation this pattern of notes occurs directly opposite one another (except on the staggered 2nd and 3rd strings). The principle here is the same as the half-step note groupings. Having isolated a simple four-note pattern, we're able to visualize its various repetitions across the fretboard using connected octave shapes.

Essentially, we could reference our note clusters around any of these notes. However, by simply targeting each B and G note across the fretboard, we've discovered associated note groupings that account for the bulk of the fretboard. In other words, from just a couple of simple four-note shapes and the way they repeat, we can basically visualize every natural note on the guitar neck!

Here's an example of the way both note groupings interact across the fretboard. Remember, it's all about creating familiar anchor points that function as visual cues when we're playing. This technique allows us to form these visual connections on the fretboard quickly and easily:

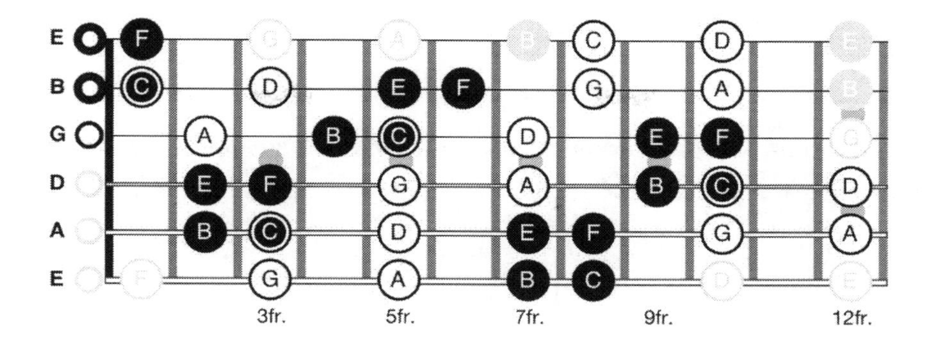

Note: Each circled C note highlights the point at which the two shapes overlap one another.

> ***Tip:*** *This visualization technique works hand in hand with the reference points established in* ***Chapter 2****. Think of it as a way to fill in the gaps. Remember, each connected octave shape also applies to any note within these floating reference points–it's all connected!*

Exercise 7

Playing through each half-step note grouping in sequence, move from the lowest position on the fretboard to the highest.

Starting at the open strings, play to a metronome and move through each of the B - C - E - F note clusters as illustrated below. Name each note aloud and keep ascending until you reach the highest point possible on the fretboard.

Example 4.1

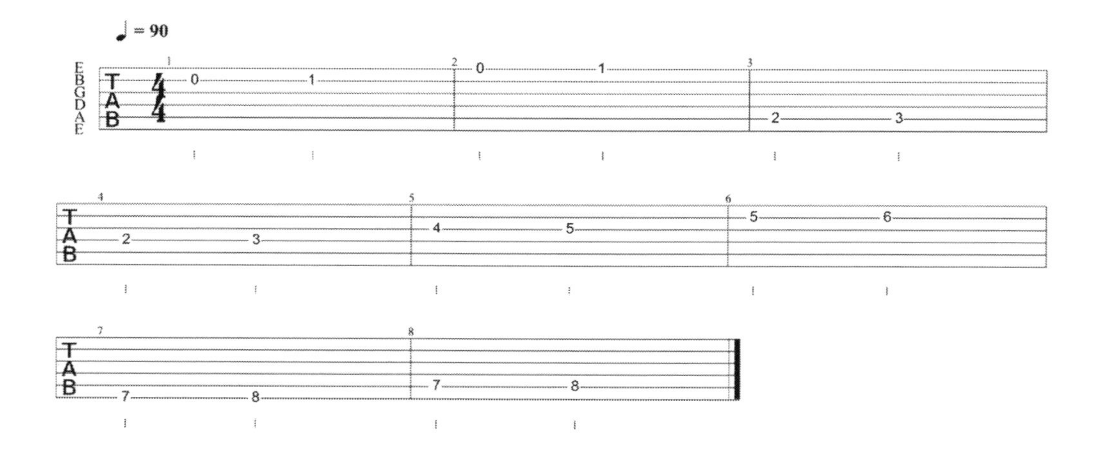

> ***Tip:*** *There are five sets of note clusters in each half of the fretboard–make sure you don't miss any.*

Exercise 8

Playing through each whole-step note grouping in sequence, move from the lowest position on the fretboard to the highest.

Starting at the open strings, play to a metronome and move through each of the G - A - C - D note clusters as illustrated below. Name each note aloud and keep ascending until you reach the highest point possible on the fretboard.

Example 4.2

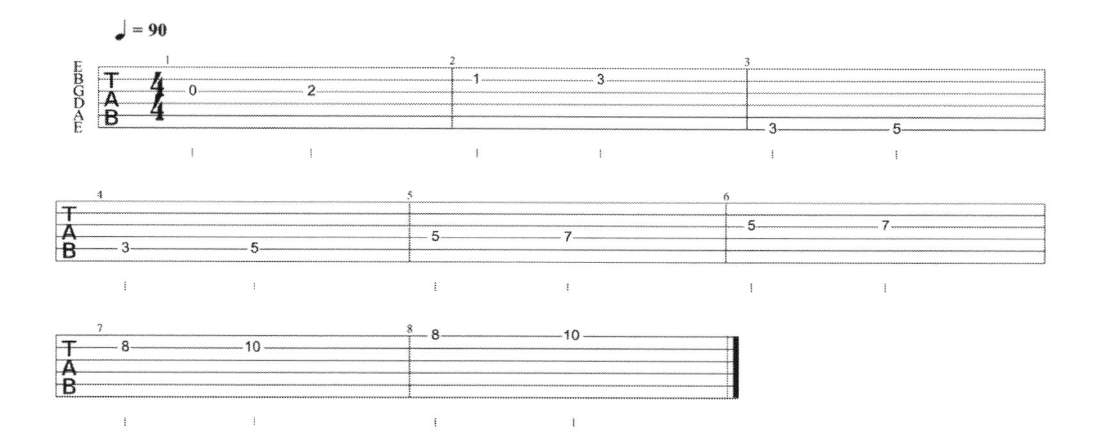

Tip: Always pay close attention to the physical space each note (or in this case, each note cluster) occupies. Try to mentally picture each note as if it were written on the fretboard.

Extra Credit

- See if you can descend the note groupings in both **Exercise 7** and **Exercise 8**, starting from their highest position on the guitar neck and playing through to their lowest.

- Try to come up with some simple melodic phrases based around the note groupings in both **Exercise 7** and **Exercise 8**. See if you can repeat these melodic patterns in each of their various positions as you ascend or descend the guitar neck.

5

Visualization & Integration

This final chapter brings together the information we've learned by integrating these concepts and techniques into real playing situations.

Repetition Is Key

In **Chapter 1** of this book, we revisited the essentials of fretboard anatomy. We simplified things down to the key elements and introduced a basic system for locating any note anywhere on the fretboard. We then moved forward in **Chapter 2** to establish key vertical anchor points in different segments of the fretboard. In **Chapter 3**, we looked at the relevance of connected octave shapes and how they can be used to dramatically extend the reach of these reference points. Lastly, in **Chapter 4** we explored a broader approach that combined these concepts, isolating floating reference points using connected shapes and note repetitions across the fretboard.

Each new section has built a comprehensive system for fretboard visualization. However, the keen observer will notice that we've essentially been dealing with the same information from different perspectives. This highlights a key aspect in the task at hand: *repetition, repetition, repetition*. Each chapter has worked toward a dynamic approach that can be integrated into the numerous ways we use the fretboard. In this final chapter, we're not introducing a new concept but are instead focusing on some tips and exercises to help apply and consolidate the things we've learned.

Tips on Memorization

As we've seen, the notes we play are a vital part of the basic language of music. Knowing them allows us to better understand and communicate the things we play on guitar. In making visual connections across the fretboard, we begin to decipher and organize this information into recognizable patterns. These patterns provide an essential framework for demystifying the fretboard puzzle.

Throughout this book, the exercises and techniques we've been working with have aimed at streamlining this process as much as possible. As you continue to explore the methods outlined, here are some key concepts to keep in mind:

- **Keep It Simple:** The fretboard isn't as overwhelming as it appears. It's a straightforward and predictable sequence of note repetitions. Focusing on key anchor points organizes this information into easily digestible sections. Establishing simple visual cues will help streamline memorization.

- **Visualize It:** Each note occupies its own unique space of fretboard real estate. The goal of memorization is to strengthen these visual associations. Try to picture each note as if it were written on the fretboard. Practice viewing notes in isolation from the linear framework of the musical alphabet.

- **Don't Rush:** Visualization exercises are designed for creating visual connections on the fretboard. The goal is to focus on what your mind is doing, not your fingers. Playing these exercises too fast can be counterproductive. Always remember, rushing this process is never a shortcut.

- **Embrace Repetition:** Memorizing the notes on the fretboard isn't a difficult task, but it's a *repetitive* one. The process of actively remembering something increases the accessibility of that information. In short, mental recall becomes faster and easier the more you do it.

- **Consistency Is Key:** Focus less on the amount of time spent and more on the *frequency* of time spent. Larger, infrequent practice sessions are significantly less effective than shorter, regular ones. Practice memorization in small but consistent chunks–snack, don't binge.

- **Mix It Up:** Practicing multiple techniques and exercises engages the same information from different perspectives. This ensures that you focus on the goal, not the method. Varying your approach better prepares you for how this information applies to real playing situations.

- **Make It a Game:** Challenges are an extremely effective learning tool. Instead of continually repeating the same exercises, create new ones. Try setting objectives, using time limits, tracking tempos, or incentivizing with rewards. These are invaluable strategies for testing and honing your skills.

- **Practice Without Playing:** Fretboard memorization is about mental recall. Visualization can be done anywhere; it doesn't require a guitar to practice. Running through exercises mentally without the guitar will maximize their effectiveness when practiced with one.

- **Practice When Playing:** Fretboard visualization shouldn't be seen as a separate task from other practice we might do. Mentally reinforcing visual connections on the fretboard while playing will enhance our spatial awareness in real-life situations. Applying this skill in context is always the end goal.

- **Test Yourself:** Anything we play can be a tool for testing our visualization skills. Stop and ask yourself: What note am I playing? What are the surrounding notes? What are the other notes in the chord or scale I'm using? How could I translate this to a different area on the fretboard? And so on.

Fretboard Worksheets

As with many things, the learning is in the *doing*. The following sections provide a short series of worksheets that require you to start putting what you've learned into practice! Notice that answers have intentionally *not* been provided. Work through each set of diagrams on your guitar and use the various techniques we've covered to cross-reference your answers. Here are some key questions that will be helpful to keep in mind:

- Where are these notes in proximity to the key reference points I've memorized?
- What are the connected octave shapes surrounding these notes?
- How are these notes related to the closest floating reference points I can see?

> ***Tip:*** *Remember, learning the fretboard isn't just about locating different notes on the guitar neck. It's also about integrating the key techniques we've learned into real playing situations.*

Note: The following exercises are provided as examples for practicing the skills we've learned. Their usefulness doesn't depend on being familiar with the exact chord or scale shapes being referred to.

Worksheet 1

Here are some movable octave shapes you should be familiar with. Name the notes associated with each shape:

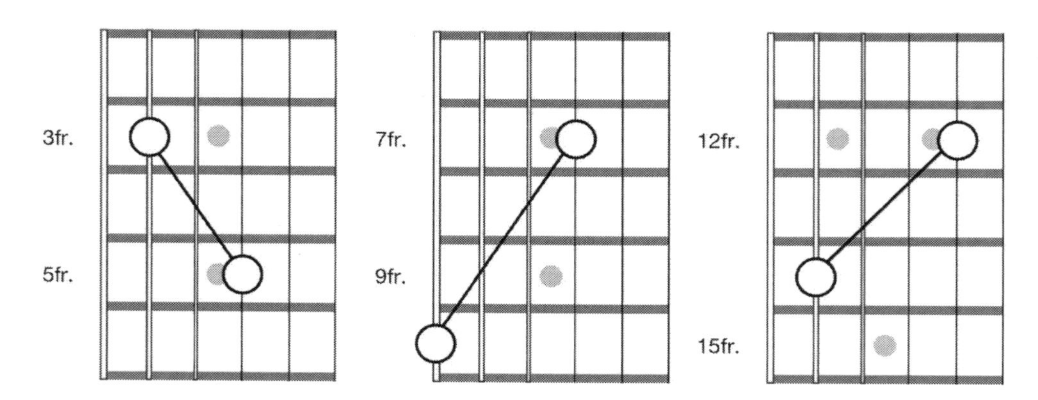

Here's an example of some basic power chords built from the 5th and 6th strings. Name the missing notes in each shape:

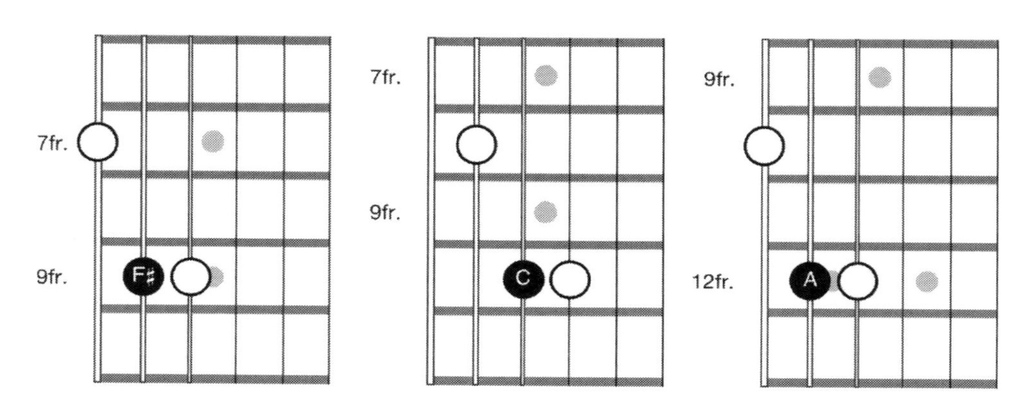

Worksheet 2

Here are some well-known major chord shapes. Name the missing notes in each shape:

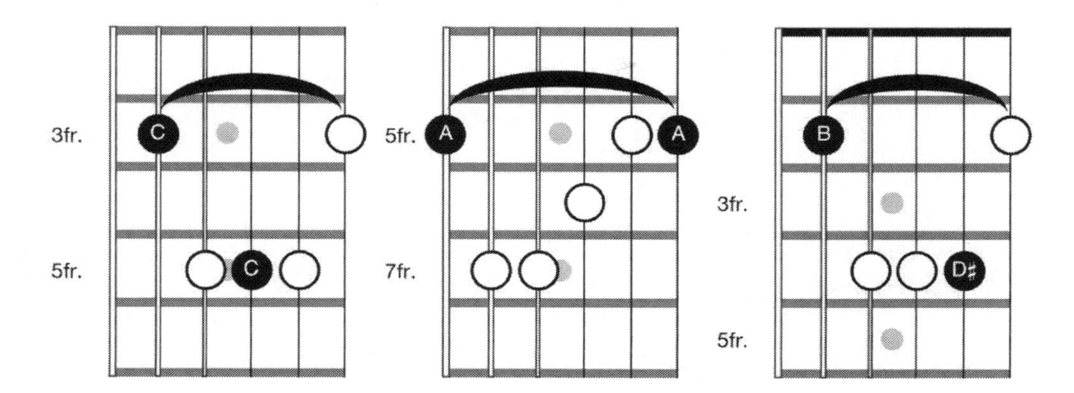

Here are some well-known minor chord shapes. Name the missing notes in each shape:

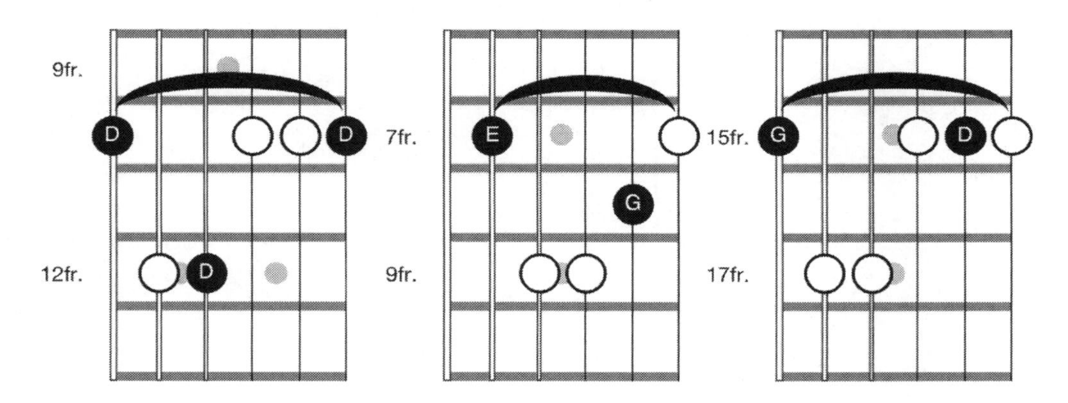

Worksheet 3

Here are some popular pentatonic scale patterns. Name the missing notes in each pattern:

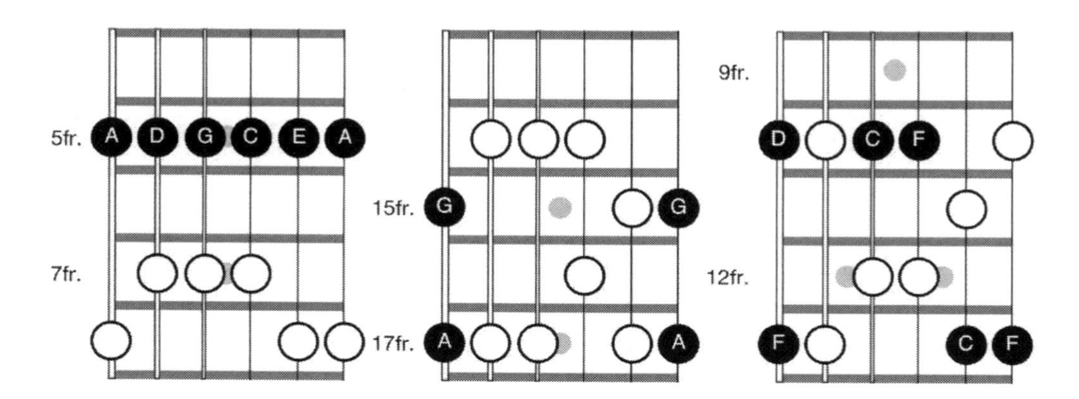

Here's a collection of notes taken from a few short guitar riffs in G major. Name the notes used in each riff:

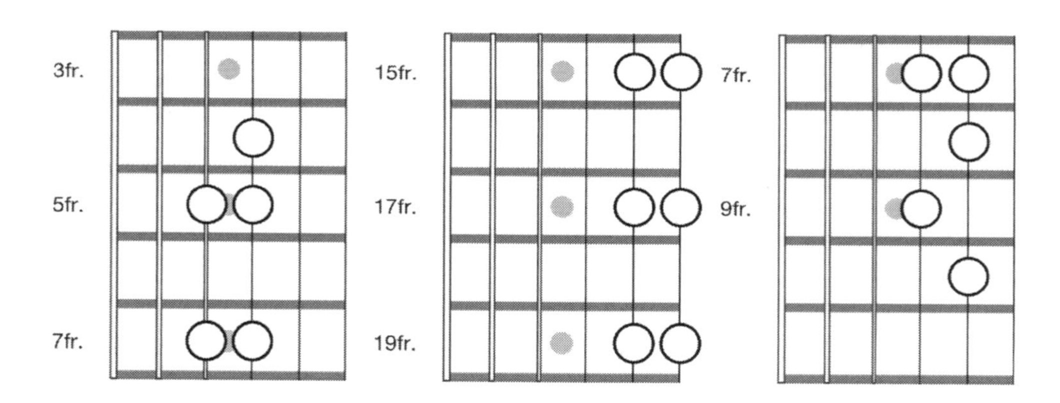

Worksheet 4

Here are some common major seventh chord shapes. Name each note within these chords:

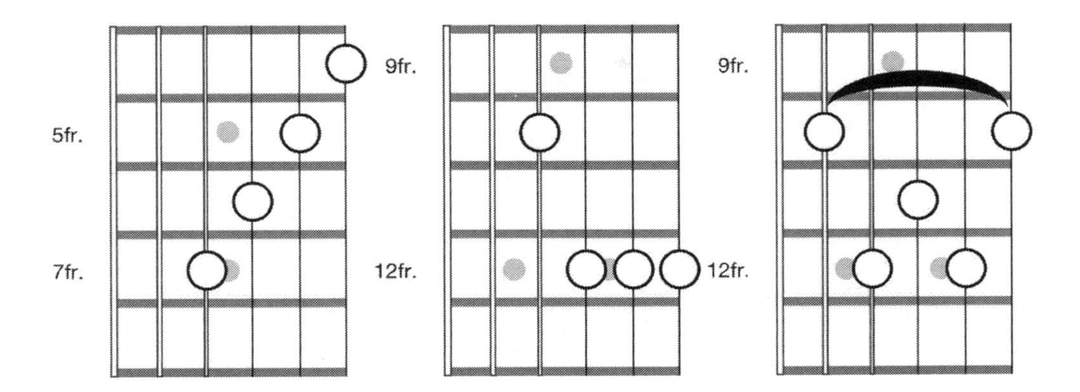

Here are some common minor seventh chord shapes. Name each note within these chords:

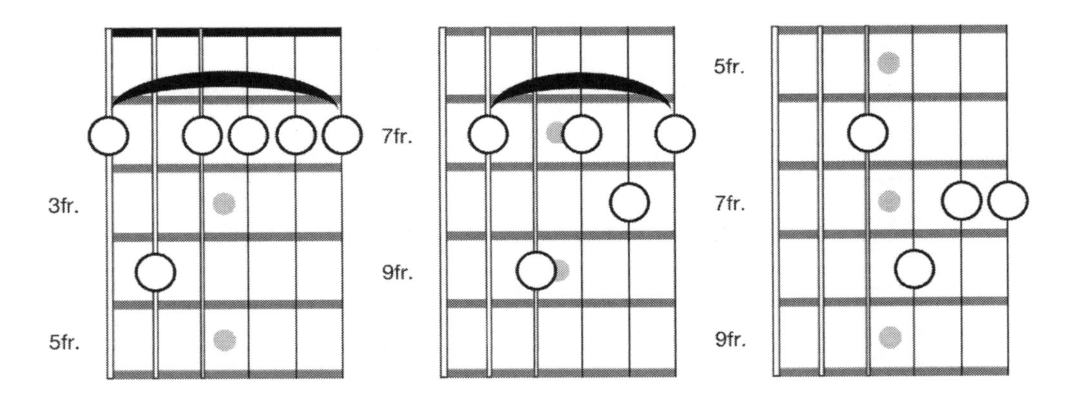

Tip: These exercises are examples of ways we can regularly test our knowledge of the guitar neck in everyday playing situations. Remember, there's no point in trying to memorize the fretboard if we don't practice applying that information when playing.

Exercise 9

Move from the 6th string to the 1st string and back again, isolating one note at a time.

Playing to a metronome and naming each note aloud, start at the 6th string and loop through every E note in the first half of the fretboard as demonstrated. Having cycled through each string, repeat this with every F, G, A, B, C, and D note in sequence.

Example 5.1

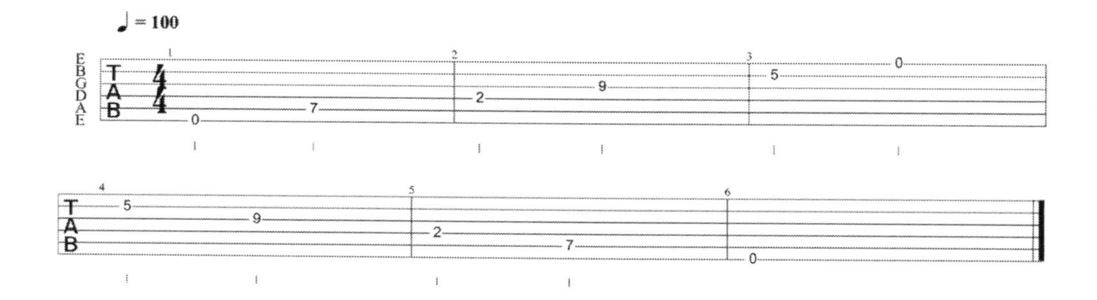

> ***Tip:*** *Each note occurs only once until the 12th fret (except on open strings). Focus on the specific position of the notes on each string. Try to visualize a note ahead of the one you're actually playing.*

Exercise 10

Practice playing and naming notes at random across the entire fretboard.

Isolate one string at a time and *without looking* randomly play a note anywhere along that string. Look at the fretboard and practice naming that note aloud before repeating this process.

Note: This exercise will now include sharps and flats. Make sure you name these aloud in reference to both natural notes on either side (e.g., "A♯ or B♭"). Because this is an improvised exercise, no illustration is needed here.

Tip: *Be conscious not just to target areas on the fretboard you know well. Make sure you attempt to balance out the random note choice both above and below the 12th fret. Allocate a small amount of time to spend on each string before moving on to the next (1 – 2 minutes, for example).*

Extra Credit

- Extend **Exercise 9** by starting it from the 12th fret. Using the upper half of the fretboard, practice cycling through each natural note of the musical alphabet in sequence.
- Remove the one-string-at-a-time limitation from **Exercise 10**. Randomly practice playing any note, in any position, on any string, naming each note aloud before moving on to the next.

Final Thoughts

Congratulations on completing ***Learn Your Fretboard***!

If you've followed each section closely to this point, you'll have an extremely solid foundation in place for fretboard visualization. The purpose of this handbook wasn't to cover every single approach to memorizing the fretboard. Instead, the goal was to highlight key strategies and exercises tailored to how we use the guitar in real playing situations. The intention has been to engage with the guitar neck from multiple perspectives and establish a system that's both comprehensive and cohesive.

The content in this book is intended to be relevant for guitar players of almost any skill level. However, like mastering any other technique on guitar, creating visual connections on the fretboard takes a bit of practice. The main difference here is that we're training our brain to keep up with our fingers, whereas the challenge is often the other way around.

Although we've covered various techniques in isolation, ultimately fretboard visualization shouldn't be viewed as a separate task from learning or playing anything else on guitar. As such, practicing these visual connections in everyday playing is always the end goal. It's my sincere hope that this simple guide has encouraged fresh revelations for beginners and experienced players alike.

May this book help inspire you toward continued learning and creativity.

Additional Resources

For more resources, including great free content, be sure to visit us at:

www.guitariq.com

Stay in touch with all the latest news. To connect with us online, head to:

www.guitariq.com/connect

Would you like to read more? For a complete list of Luke's books, check out:

www.guitariq.com/books

Remember to grab your online bonus! Get the free bonus content for this book at:

www.guitariq.com/lyf-bonus

Interested in a master class with Luke? To check out his online workshops, go to:

www.guitariq.com/academy

About the Author

Having played for over 25 years, Luke Zecchin is an accomplished guitarist with a wealth of studio and live experience. Outside his work teaching music, Luke has toured extensively alongside renowned national and international acts, performing at everything from clubs, theaters, and festivals to various appearances on commercial radio and national television.

Playing lead guitar, Luke has worked on projects with established international producers and engineers. He has been fortunate to see these collaborations break into both the Top 50 ARIA Album and Singles charts, having also received nationwide airplay and notable debuts on the Australian iTunes Rock charts.

As the founder of **GuitarIQ.com**, Luke is dedicated to the education and coaching of guitar players all over the globe. With books available in over 100 countries worldwide, he has emerged as an international chart-topping author in his field.

Luke continues to work as an author and musician from his project studio based in the Adelaide Hills, South Australia.

Find him online at **LukeZecchin.com**.

Liked This Book?

Did you find this book useful? You can make a big difference in helping us spread the word!

While it would be nice to have the promotional muscle of a major publishing house, independent authors rely heavily on the loyalty of their audience. Online reviews are one of the most powerful tools we have for getting attention and finding new readers.

If you found this book helpful, please consider helping us by leaving an online review at your place of purchase. Reviews needn't be long or in-depth; a star rating with a short comment is perfect. If you could take a minute to leave your feedback, it would be sincerely appreciated!

23173117R00033

Made in the USA
San Bernardino, CA
22 January 2019